THE
ENGLISH BISCUIT
AND
COOKIE BOOK
· SONIA ALLISON ·

"Recipes for such old dears as Digestive Biscuits, Cornish Fairings and Madeira Fingers make this a bully of a cookie cookbook."

—Iris Ihde Frey, author of
Crumpets and Scones

"The recipes in Sonia Allison's book are cleverly arranged for easy reading and following.

Anyone who loves to bake or is just a beginner, will find good use for this book. . . .

I highly recommend Sonia Allison's book."

—Bess Hoffman, author of
Cookies by Bess

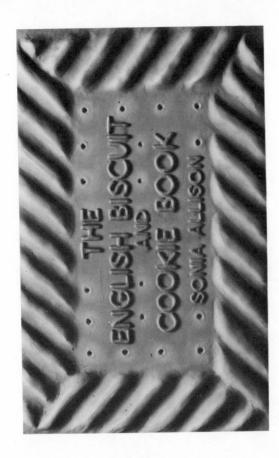

THE ENGLISH BISCUIT AND COOKIE BOOK

· SONIA ALLISON ·

St. Martin's Press New York

Jacket design and photograph by
Marjorie Dressler.
Biscuit created by Karen Sutch
and G. Clark Sealy III.

THE ENGLISH BISCUIT AND COOKIE BOOK. Copyright © 1983 by Sonia Allison. All
rights reserved. Printed in the United States of America. No part of this book may be
used or reproduced in any manner whatsoever without written permission except in the
case of brief quotations embodied in critical articles or reviews. For information,
address St. Martin's Press, 175 Fifth Avenue, New York, N.Y. 10010.

Design by Laura Hammond

Library of Congress Cataloging in Publication Data

Allison, Sonia.
    The English biscuit and cookie book.

    Includes index.
    1. Cookies.   I. Title.
TX772.A38   1983   641.8'654   83-8691
ISBN 0-312-25347-8

10 9 8 7 6 5 4 3

CONTENTS

INTRODUCTION

"Polly put the kettle on, we'll all have tea."
—*Charles Dickens, Barnaby Rudge*

The biscuit tin is to the English what the cookie jar is to Americans, and no British household would be complete without a store of assorted biscuits on hand for nibbling, as the mood takes one, with midmorning coffee, afternoon tea, and a late night drink of milk or chocolate to soothe away the cares of the day and induce sweet dreams laced with sugar and spice and maybe a sprinkling of nuts for good measure!

In many respects, afternoon tea is synonymous with England. This unique institution of ours, supposedly "invented" by the Duchess of Bedford, was later embroidered by Queen Victoria into a rich, colorful, and delicious tapestry of cakes, buns, and biscuits, many named after Albert, her beloved Consort—a veritable feast of a meal for adults and children alike.

Customs and traditions of yesteryear may have changed with the passing of time, but in England as in America, devotion and loyalty to biscuits and cookies remains steadfast. There is nothing more welcoming to come home to than the warming, fragrant, and tempting aroma of freshly baked goodies, be they a simple style of refrigerator cookie—which we have borrowed from America—or buttery and meltingly tender shortbreads, so characteristic of a British Christmas.

—*Sonia Allison, Bushey, Hertfordshire*

TIPS

1. Do not alter the quantities given in the recipes or substitute different fats or sugars for the ones recommended.

2. Keep to the oven temperature stated. In general, you will do *less* harm if you reduce, rather than increase, the temperature.

3. Use a mixing bowl that is large enough to take all the ingredients and still enable you to work freely without the ingredients flying out over the top.

4. Place the biscuits on a shallow cookie sheet, as one with high sides shields the biscuits around the edges from even heat.

5. Most biscuits should be left on the trays for 2 to 3 minutes before being transferred to a wire cooling rack.

6. Biscuits should be left until they are completely cold before being stored in an airtight container. If not, they will soften.

7. Cakes and biscuits should *never* be stored in the same container. If put together, the biscuits will soften.

8. Where necessary, individual hints and tips are included within the recipes.

ROLLED BISCUITS

FRUIT 'N' NUT OATCAKES (Makes 16)

These not-too-sweet English biscuits team very well with cheese at the end of a meal, or make an unusual mid-morning snack.

3/4 cup whole-wheat flour
1/2 teaspoon salt
1/2 teaspoon baking powder
1/4 cup butter or margarine
1 cup oatmeal
1/4 cup dates or pitted
   prunes, finely chopped
1/4 cup walnuts, finely
   chopped
1 small egg, beaten
Cold water to mix, if
   necessary

1. Sift the flour, salt, and baking powder into a bowl. Rub in the butter or margarine until the mixture is finely blended.

2. Add the oatmeal, dates or prunes, and the nuts. Mix the ingredients well.

3. Mix to a stiff dough with beaten egg and water if necessary.

4. Turn onto a floured surface. Knead lightly until smooth.

5. Roll out fairly thinly and cut into 16 rounds with a 2-inch cookie cutter.

6. Transfer to greased cookie sheets. Bake until lightly browned, allowing about 25 minutes in an oven preheated to 350°F (180°C).

7. Cool on a wire rack. Store in an airtight tin when cold.

2 cups all-purpose flour
1/2 teaspoon salt
1/2 cup butter or margarine
1/2 cup granulated sugar
1 teaspoon vanilla extract
3 to 4 tablespoons beaten egg

PLAIN BISCUITS

(Makes 24)

In this recipe the biscuits have all been cut into rounds, but there is nothing to stop you from using any shape of cutter you fancy to suit the occasion. From one basic recipe, you can make endless variations and produce an assortment to please everybody.

1. Sift the flour and salt into a bowl. Rub in the butter or margarine until the mixture resembles fine breadcrumbs.

2. Add the sugar. Mix to a stiff paste with extract and beaten egg, using a fork to draw the mixture together.

3. Turn onto a floured surface. Knead lightly until smooth.

4. Wrap in foil or plastic wrap. Refrigerate for 30 minutes.

5. Roll out thinly and cut into 24 rounds, re-rolling and re-cutting trimmings to give the required number.

6. Transfer to lightly greased cookie sheets and bake for 12 to 15 minutes in an oven preheated to 350°F (180°C). When ready, the biscuits should be a light gold color.

7. Transfer to a wire rack to cool. Store in an airtight tin when cold.

CINNAMON BISCUITS (*Makes 24*)

Make as Plain Biscuits, sifting 2 teaspoons cinnamon with the flour and salt.

LEMON BISCUITS (*Makes 24*)

Make as Plain Biscuits, adding 2 teaspoons finely grated lemon peel with the sugar.

ORANGE BISCUITS (*Makes 24*)

Make as Plain Biscuits, adding 2 teaspoons finely grated orange peel with the sugar.

ALMOND BISCUITS (*Makes 30*)

Make as Plain Biscuits, adding 4 tablespoons ground almonds with the sugar. Substitute almond extract for vanilla.

CURRANT BISCUITS (*Makes 24*)

Make as Plain Biscuits, adding 3 tablespoons currants with the sugar.

COCONUT BISCUITS

(Makes 24)

Make as Plain Biscuits, adding ¼ cup dried flaked coconut with the sugar.

CHOCOLATE BISCUITS

(Makes 24)

Make as Plain Biscuits, substituting 2 tablespoons cocoa powder for 2 tablespoons flour. Use brown sugar instead of granulated sugar.

GINGER BISCUITS

(Makes 24)

Make as Plain Biscuits, sifting 2 teaspoons powdered ginger with the flour and salt. Use brown sugar instead of white, and omit the vanilla extract.

COFFEE BISCUITS

(Makes 24)

Make as Plain Biscuits, sifting 1 tablespoon instant coffee powder with the flour and salt. Omit the vanilla extract.

MADEIRA FINGERS (Makes 36)

These are elegant, old–world–style biscuits that can be served with coffee, for afternoon tea, or used to accompany desserts. They came about in the last century, the result of a happy friendship between England and Portugal.

1½ cups all-purpose flour
Pinch of salt
½ cup butter
⅜ cup granulated sugar
2 to 3 tablespoons Madeira wine

Topping
  Beaten egg
  Extra granulated sugar

1. Sift the flour and salt into a bowl. Rub in the butter until the mixture resembles fine breadcrumbs.

2. Add the sugar. Mix to a stiff paste with the Madeira, using a fork to draw the mixture together.

3. Wrap in foil or plastic wrap and refrigerate for 30 minutes.

4. Turn onto a floured surface and knead lightly until smooth. Roll out thinly and prick all over with the prongs of a fork.

5. Cut into approximately 36 fingers measuring 1 × 2½ inches.

6. Transfer to lightly greased cookie sheets. Brush with beaten egg and sprinkle each finger with a little sugar.

7. Bake for about 15 minutes in an oven preheated to 375°F (190°C). When ready, the biscuits should be a light gold color.

8. Cool on a wire rack. Store in an airtight tin when cold.

3/4 cup whole-wheat flour
1/4 cup all-purpose flour
1/2 teaspoon baking powder
1 tablespoon oatmeal
4 tablespoons butter
4 tablespoons brown sugar
3 to 4 tablespoons cold
    milk

DIGESTIVE BISCUITS

(Makes 12)

Traditional midmorning and very British biscuits, digestives are also delicious buttered and served with cheese. For Chocolate Digestives, brush the undersides of the biscuits with melted bittersweet or milk chocolate after baking.

1. Sift the flours and baking powder into a bowl. Add the oatmeal.

2. Rub in the butter. Add the sugar. Run the mixture through the fingers to mix well.

3. Using a fork, stir in the milk to form a stiff paste.

4. Turn onto a floured surface. Knead lightly until smooth. Roll out thinly.

5. Cut into 12 rounds with a 2½-inch cookie cutter, re-rolling and re-cutting trimmings to make the required number.

6. Transfer to greased cookie sheets and prick all over with a fork.

7. Bake until pale gold, allowing 15 to 18 minutes in an oven preheated to 375°F (190°C).

8. Cool on a wire rack. Store in an airtight tin when cold.

SHREWSBURY BISCUITS (Makes 5)

Shrewsbury, a town on the border of England and Wales, lends its name to these biscuits, which date back to the mid-seventeenth century. They were originally known as cakes and were much more elaborate than modern-day versions, containing caraway seeds, sherry, nutmeg, and rose water.

2 cups all-purpose flour
½ cup butter or margarine
½ cup granulated sugar
Finely shredded peel of 1
  washed and dried small
  lemon
1 small egg, well beaten
7 to 8 teaspoons cold milk

Topping
  Extra granulated sugar

1. Sift the flour into a bowl. Rub in the butter or margarine. Mix in the sugar and lemon peel.

2. Using a fork, mix in the egg and milk to form a fairly stiff dough.

3. Turn onto a floured surface and knead lightly until smooth.

4. Roll out thinly and, to keep to the traditional style, cut into five 5-inch rounds, using a small plate as a guide.

5. Transfer to greased cookie sheets. Bake for 15 to 20 minutes in an oven preheated to 350°F (180°C). When ready, the biscuits should be light gold in color.

6. Dredge with sugar. Cool on a wire rack. Store in an airtight tin when cold.

Chocolate Squares

(Makes 20)

Make as Shrewsbury Biscuits, but reduce the quantity of flour to 1¾ cups and add ¼ cup cocoa powder in its place. Sift both together into a bowl. Omit the lemon peel and flavor with 1 teaspoon vanilla extract, adding it at the same time as the egg. Roll out thinly and cut into 20 squares. Bake as Shrewsbury Biscuits. Dust with sifted confectioners' sugar. Store in an airtight tin.

Chocolate Sandwich Biscuits

(Makes 10)

Make as Chocolate Squares. Sift confectioners' sugar over 10 biscuits. Spread remainder with homemade or store-bought chocolate spread or cake frosting. Place two halves carefully together with sugar side uppermost. Store in an airtight tin. If you like, seek out Nutella, an Italian chocolate nut spread available at some gourmet stores.

RASPBERRY SANDWICH BISCUITS (Makes 10)

These colorful biscuits are best made and eaten on the same day. They are very popular with English children at birthday parties.

1. Sift the flour into a bowl. Cut in the butter or margarine with a knife and rub in finely with the fingertips.

2. Mix in the sugar and almonds.

3. Using a fork, mix to a stiff dough with the egg.

4. Turn onto a floured surface. Knead lightly until smooth.

5. Roll out thinly. Cut into 20 rounds with a 2-inch cookie cutter, re-rolling and re-cutting trimmings to give the full quantity.

6. Transfer to a lightly buttered cookie sheet. Bake for 12 minutes in an oven preheated to 400°F (200°C).

7. Remove from the oven. Cool on the sheet for about 3 minutes. Carefully transfer biscuits to a wire cooling rack.

8. When completely cold, sandwich together with a thin spread of jam. Dust with confectioners' sugar.

1 cup all-purpose flour
¼ cup butter or margarine
¼ cup granulated sugar
2 tablespoons ground almonds
1 medium egg, well beaten

To complete
Raspberry jam
Confectioners' sugar

1 cup all-purpose flour
⅝ cup semolina flour
¾ cup confectioners' sugar
⅝ cup butter or margarine
½ teaspoon vanilla or
    almond extract
1 small egg, well beaten

CHRISTMAS STARS

(Makes 30)

Short, crisp biscuits that are well suited to the festive season. The English enjoy them with a glass of sherry on Christmas Eve.

1. Sift the dry ingredients into a bowl. Rub in the butter or margarine finely.

2. Mix to a stiff pastry with extract and egg, using a fork to bind the ingredients together. Wrap in foil or plastic wrap and chill for 45 minutes.

3. Turned onto a floured surface. Knead lightly until smooth. Roll out thinly and cut into 30 stars with a cookie cutter, re-rolling and re-cutting trimmings to get the required number.

4. Transfer to a lightly greased cookie sheet and bake for about 15 to 20 minutes in an oven preheated to 350°F (180°C). When ready, the biscuits should be straw-colored.

5. Cool on a wire rack. Store in an airtight tin when cold.

ICED CHRISTMAS STARS

(Makes 30)

For glacé icing, sift 1 cup confectioners' sugar into a bowl. Mix to a stiff icing with a few teaspoons lemon juice. Spread thinly over the biscuits. If you wish, sprinkle the icing with toasted coconut or chopped nuts. Leave until set before eating or storing.

CHRISTMAS BISCUITS

(Makes 14)

With the warm aroma of sugar and spice and all things nice, these are delicious English biscuits for any festive season. They are particularly recommended for Halloween, Christmas, and even Easter.

1. Sift the flour, allspice, and cinnamon into a bowl.

2. Cut in the butter or margarine with a knife and then rub it in with the fingertips.

3. Stir in the sugar. Using a fork, mix to a stiff dough with the egg.

4. Draw the mixture together with the fingertips. Turn out onto a floured surface. Knead lightly until smooth.

5. Roll out thinly. Cut into about 14 biscuits with assorted shaped cutters, re-rolling and re-cutting trimmings to give the required number.

6. Transfer to a lightly greased cookie sheet. Bake for 12 minutes in an oven preheated to 400°F (200°C).

7. Cool for a few minutes; then transfer to a wire cooling rack. Store in an airtight container when completely cold.

1 cup all-purpose flour
2 teaspoons allspice
1 teaspoon cinnamon
¼ cup butter or margarine
¼ cup brown sugar
1 medium egg, well beaten

UNROLLED BISCUITS

MACAROON CRUNCHIES

(Makes 12)

Lovely thin biscuits laced with ground almonds and thick honey; a great favorite in England.

1 egg white from large egg
4 drops almond extract
4 tablespoons ground
   almonds
¼ cup granulated sugar
1 tablespoon honey
1 tablespoon ground rice or
   semolina flour

Topping
6 whole blanched almonds,
   split

1. Line cookie sheets with wax paper or foil. Alternatively, use nonstick sheets.

2. Place all the ingredients, except the split almonds, in a bowl. Beat until well mixed.

3. Drop teaspoonfuls of the mixture onto the prepared sheets. Place them well apart since they spread. Put half an almond on each.

4. Bake for 15 to 20 minutes in an oven preheated to 325°F (160°C). When ready, the biscuits should be pale gold in color and firm on top.

5. Lift carefully onto a wire rack and leave until cold. Store in an airtight tin.

HONEY CRUNCHIES   *(Makes 30)*

Adaptable little biscuits-cum-cakes that are ideal for coffee mornings and children's parties.

5 tablespoons clear honey
3/8 cup butter or margarine
2 teaspoons instant coffee powder
1 tablespoon hot water
1½ cups sifted confectioners' sugar
3½ cups cornflakes or puffed rice breakfast cereal

1. Melt the honey and butter or margarine in a saucepan. Remove from the heat.

2. Dissolve the coffee powder in the hot water.

3. Add the coffee, sugar, and cornflakes to the saucepan.

4. Mix well so that all the cornflakes are coated with the honey mixture and hold together.

5. Spoon into 30 paper cupcake liners and leave in a cool place to set.

Note
If possible, make and eat these biscuits on the same day. They lose their crispness fairly quickly, especially in warm weather.

2¾ cups desiccated (dry
    flaked) coconut
1⅛ cup granulated sugar
½ teaspoon vanilla or
    almond extract
2 medium eggs

COCONUT PYRAMIDS

(Makes 24)

The recipe for these Pyramids, or Coconut Macaroons as they are sometimes called, is richly endowed with eggs. These biscuits are well appreciated during the Jewish observance of Passover, when the use of flour in cooking is not permitted.

1. Line 2 cookie sheets with rice paper or aluminum foil. Grease foil but not rice paper.

2. Mix together the coconut, sugar, extract, and eggs, lightly beaten.

3. Shape into 24 pyramids and place on prepared sheets.

4. Bake for about 15 minutes in an oven preheated to 350°F (180°C). When ready, the pyramids should be a warm gold color.

5. Remove from the sheets with a spatula, trim away surplus rice paper (if used) from the bottom of each, and cool on wire racks. Store in an airtight tin when cold.

CHOCNUT COOKIES (Makes 20)

Easy-to-make biscuits, studded with chocolate chips and walnuts and flavored with vanilla.

3/8 cup butter or margarine, softened
3/8 cup granulated sugar
3/8 cup brown sugar
1 teaspoon vanilla extract
1 medium egg, beaten
1½ cups self-rising flour
½ cup walnuts, coarsely chopped
½ cup chocolate chips

1. Cream the butter or margarine and the sugars together until light and fluffy.

2. Beat in the extract and egg. Using a fork, mix in the flour, walnuts, and chocolate chips.

3. Divide the mixture into 20 pieces and roll into balls. Place them well apart on lightly greased cookie sheets because they spread.

4. Bake for about 12 to 15 minutes in an oven preheated to 350°F (180°C). When ready, the biscuits should be pale gold color.

5. Cool on wire racks. Store in an airtight container when cold.

CHOCNUT SPICE COOKIES

(Makes 20)

Sift 1 to 2 teaspoons of allspice with the flour. Otherwise, follow the recipe for Chocnut Cookies exactly.

CHOCNUT GINGER COOKIES

(Makes 20)

Halve the quantity of nuts to 1/4 cup and add 1 tablespoon finely chopped candied ginger. Otherwise, follow the recipe for Chocnut Cookies exactly.

CHOC-CHERRY COOKIES

(Makes 20)

Replace nuts with 1/4 cup finely chopped candied cherries. Otherwise, follow the recipe for Chocnut Cookies exactly.

MELTING MOMENTS

(*Makes 20 to 24*)

Traditionally British oat-covered biscuits that, as their name suggests, are deliciously short and melting as you bite into them. And they are easy to make!

1. Cream the butter and sugar until very soft and light in texture and color.

2. Beat in the egg yolk and vanilla extract.

3. Sift the flour, cornstarch, and salt together and, using a fork, work into the butter-sugar mixture.

4. Shape into 20 to 24 small balls, each about the size of a marble.

5. Toss each ball in the oats.

6. Transfer to 2 greased cookie sheets, leaving plenty of room between each biscuit so they can spread.

7. Bake until pale gold, allowing 15 to 20 minutes in an oven preheated to 375°F (190°C).

8. Cool on a wire rack. Store in an airtight tin when cold.

½ cup butter, softened
⅜ cup granulated sugar
1 egg yolk from medium egg
1 teaspoon vanilla extract
1 cup self-rising flour
2 tablespoons cornstarch
¼ teaspoon salt
Rolled oats

1/2 cup butter
1/2 cup brown sugar
1 medium egg, beaten
3 tablespoons clear honey
1/2 teaspoon vanilla extract
2 cups self-rising flour,
 sifted

HONEY COOKIES

(Makes 36)

Chewy cookies that, like many others in this book, need no rolling out.

1. Cream the butter and sugar together until light and fluffy.

2. Beat in the egg, honey, and extract.

3. Fork in the flour to form a soft paste.

4. Using a teaspoon, place small mounds of the mixture on 3 greased and floured cookie sheets, keeping the mounds well apart because these cookies spread.

5. Press the mounds flat with damp fingers and then bake until light brown, allowing 10 to 12 minutes in an oven preheated to 350°F (180°C).

6. Cool to lukewarm, then transfer to wire racks. Store in an airtight tin when completely cold.

FRUIT AND SPICE HONEY COOKIES

(Makes 36)

Make as Honey Cookies but add 1/2 cup raisins with the extract. Sift flour with 1 teaspoon allspice.

CORNISH FAIRINGS   (Makes 24)

I always associate these crisp, spicy biscuits with very happy holidays spent in Cornwall, a picturesque region in the extreme southwest of England known for its rugged, captivating shoreline, Riviera-like summer climate, and endless tales of romance, mystery, and once-upon-a-time smuggling!

1½ *cups all-purpose flour*
1 *teaspoon soda*
1½ *teaspoons allspice*
½ *cup butter*
½ *cup brown sugar*
1½ *teaspoons corn syrup*

1. Sift the flour, soda, and spice into a bowl.

2. Place the remaining ingredients in a saucepan. Heat slowly until the butter, sugar, and syrup melt.

3. Using a fork, gently pour the melted mixture onto the dry ingredients and mix well.

4. Shape the mixture into 24 balls. Transfer to 3 buttered cookie sheets, leaving plenty of room between each ball because they spread.

5. Bake until a warm gold color, allowing about 15 minutes in an oven preheated to 375°F (190°C).

6. Cool to lukewarm, then transfer to a wire rack. Store in an airtight tin when cold.

8 squares milk chocolate
   (8 ounces)
3/8 cup butter or margarine
1/4 cup granulated sugar
1/4 cup cooking dates, finely
   chopped
5 1/4 cups cornflakes or puffed
   rice breakfast cereal

MILKY CHOC CRISPS

(Makes 24)

Marvelous uncooked biscuits that are ideal for children's parties—and not too bad for the grown-ups either!

1. Brush a jelly-roll pan, 11 × 7 inches, with melted shortening. Line the base with wax paper or aluminum foil. Brush with more shortening.

2. Break up the chocolate. Place it in a basin standing over a pan of hot water. Leave until melted, stirring once or twice.

3. Spread the melted chocolate over the base of the jelly roll pan, completely covering the paper or foil.

4. Melt butter or margarine in a saucepan. Stir in the sugar and dates. Cook gently for about 5 minutes or until the mixture becomes sticky.

5. Stir in the cornflakes. Spread the mixture evenly into the pan over the chocolate. Cool. Refrigerate when cold to firm the mixture.

6. Cut into 24 squares and lift carefully away from the paper. Store in an airtight tin.

Tip
If there is any leftover mixture, spoon into paper cupcake liners and refrigerate until firm.

FLAPJACK

(Makes 16)

I have yet to discover the origin of the name, but the recipe started life during the first World War when eggs were short—or so the story goes.

½ cup butter, softened
2 tablespoons granulated sugar
⅜ cup corn syrup
2¼ cups quick-cooking oatmeal
Large pinch salt

1. Butter a large square pan measuring about 9 × 9 × 2 inches.

2. Cream the butter and sugar until very light and pale in color.

3. Stir in the syrup, oatmeal, and salt. Spread evenly into the prepared pan.

4. Bake for about 40 minutes in an oven preheated to 350°F (180°C), or until the Flapjack is a deep gold color.

5. Remove from the oven and cut into 16 squares or strips. Leave in the tin until cold before removing.

6. Store in an airtight tin.

2 cups self-rising flour
½ cup butter
½ cup granulated sugar
3 squares dark chocolate (3
    ounces), coarsely
    chopped
1 medium egg, beaten
2 tablespoons cold strong
    coffee
2 to 3 tablespoons milk

MOCHA COOKIES

(Makes 16)

These cookies are a cross between an English biscuit and a baby fruit-bun.

1. Sift the flour into a bowl. Rub in the butter until the mixture resembles fine breadcrumbs. Add the sugar and chocolate.

2. Using a fork, mix to a stiff consistency with the egg, coffee, and milk.

3. Spoon 16 small mounds of the mixture onto 2 greased cookie sheets, leaving space between each to allow them to spread.

4. Bake until they are golden brown, allowing about 20 minutes in an oven preheated to 400°F (200°C).

5. Transfer to a wire cooling rack. Store in an airtight tin when cold.

DUTCH CINNAMON BISCUITS   (Makes 12)

These biscuits are beautifully tender and have a lovely spicy flavor.

½ cup butter, preferably unsalted

¼ cup granulated sugar

1½ cups all-purpose flour

½ teaspoon cinnamon

Topping
1 medium egg, beaten

2 tablespoons blanched almonds, finely chopped

1 tablespoon granulated sugar

1. Cream the butter and sugar together until light and fluffy.

2. Sift the flour and cinnamon and, using a fork, add to the butter mixture.

3. Spread the mixture evenly into an ungreased jelly-roll pan measuring 11 × 7 inches.

4. Brush with beaten egg and then prick lightly all over with a fork.

5. Sprinkle with almonds and sugar. Bake until golden brown in an oven preheated to 350°F (180°C). Allow approximately 20 to 25 minutes.

6. Remove from the oven and cool for 5 minutes. Cut into 12 fingers.

7. Remove from the pan when lukewarm and transfer to a wire cooling rack. Store in an airtight tin when cold.

5/8 cup butter, preferably
    unsalted
1/2 cup granulated sugar
1 3/4 cups all-purpose flour
    Pinch of salt
1/2 teaspoon vanilla extract

Topping
    Confectioners' sugar for
    dusting

DUTCH SPRITZ BISCUITS

(Makes 15)

The word "spritz," loosely translated, means to squirt, and these biscuits are piped or "squirted" onto cookie sheets in finger-length lines, S-shapes, or zigzags. They are pretty biscuits for special occasions.

1. Cream the butter with the sugar until light and fluffy.

2. Sift the flour with the salt and stir into the butter mixture. Stir in the vanilla extract. Mix thoroughly to combine.

3. Transfer the mixture to a piping bag fitted with a large, star-shaped tube.

4. Pipe about 15 lines, S-shapes, zigzags, or round whorls onto a buttered cookie sheet.

5. Bake until very pale gold, allowing about 30 to 40 minutes in an oven preheated to 300°F (150°C).

6. Leave on the sheets for 3 or 4 minutes and then transfer carefully to a wire cooling rack. Store in an airtight tin when cold. Sprinkle with confectioners' sugar before serving.

CHOCOLATE SPRITZ

(Makes 15)

If you like, dip half of each Spritz into melted bittersweet chocolate. Leave to set. Store in an airtight tin. Sprinkle with sugar lightly before serving.

PEANUT BUTTER FLAKES

(Makes 24)

Distinctively flavored, these biscuits have a very crisp, light texture.

1. Sift the flour and soda onto a plate.

2. Cream the butter or margarine with both sugars until light and fluffy. Beat in the vanilla extract, peanut butter, and the egg.

3. Using a fork, gradually work the flour mixture into the creamed ingredients.

4. Drop teaspoonfuls of mixture, 1 inch apart, onto 2 or 3 ungreased cookie sheets.

5. Bake for 10 to 12 minutes until golden in an oven preheated to 350°F (180°C).

6. Transfer to a wire rack to cool. Store in an airtight tin when cold.

½ cup all-purpose flour
¼ teaspoon soda
¼ cup butter or margarine
1½ tablespoons granulated
   sugar
¼ cup light brown sugar
½ teaspoon vanilla extract
4 tablespoons cream-style
   peanut butter
1 medium egg

SHORTBREAD SELECTION

There are many kinds of this traditional biscuit, which originated in Scotland, and given below is a selection of recipes from which to choose. Usually *no liquid is added* to bind the ingredients together.

BUTTER FINGERS

(Makes 24)

Trouble-free to make, these biscuits are reminiscent of the very best shortbreads both in taste and texture.

½ cup butter, softened
¼ cup granulated sugar
1¼ cups all-purpose flour

Topping
Extra granulated sugar

1. Cream the butter and sugar until very light and fluffy.

2. Stir in the flour with a fork. Spread evenly into an ungreased jelly-roll pan measuring 11 × 7 inches.

3. Ridge into lines, lengthwise, using the prongs of a fork.

4. Bake until pale gold, allowing 20 to 25 minutes in an oven preheated to 350°F (180°C).

5. Cool to lukewarm in the pan, then dredge lightly with sugar. Cut into 24 fingers and remove to a wire cooling rack. Store in an airtight tin when cold.

BUTTER SHORTBREAD   (8 wedges)

This is a good basic recipe from which to make delicious, crisp Scottish-style shortbread.

1. Sift the flour into a bowl. Stir in the semolina and sugar.

2. Add the butter. Cut it in with a knife and then rub in with the fingertips.

3. Draw the mixture together; it will be crumbly. Transfer to an ungreased 7-inch-round cake pan.

4. Press out smoothly until the tin is covered with an even layer of biscuit mixture.

5. Spread evenly with a spatula. Ridge the edges with a fork and then prick all over at regular intervals to give a typical shortbread effect. Sprinkle with sugar.

6. Bake for 1 hour in an oven preheated to 300°F (150°C). The shortbread should be the color of straw.

7. Remove from the oven. Cool to lukewarm and then cut into 8 wedges. Carefully ease out of the pan.

1¼ cups all-purpose flour
2 tablespoons semolina flour
    (for added crispness)
¼ cup granulated sugar
½ cup unsalted butter
Topping
4 teaspoons granulated
    sugar

8. Transfer to a wire cooling rack. When completely cold, put into an airtight container.

BUTTER SHORTBREAD WITH ALMONDS

(8 wedges)

Make as Butter Shortbread with semolina, but add ¼ cup finely ground blanched and toasted almonds with the sugar.

MELT-IN-THE-MOUTH SHORTBREAD

(8 wedges)

The ingredients are exactly the same as for Butter Shortbread but the method is different and the result is a much smoother shortbread with a melt-in-the-mouth texture. Sift the flour into a bowl. Add the semolina. In a separate bowl, cream the sugar with slightly softened butter until very light and fluffy and pale cream in color. The consistency should resemble whipped cream. Fork in the flour. When the mixture has been evenly mixed, spread it into a cake pan and continue exactly as directed for Butter Shortbread.

DUTCH SHORTBREAD

(10 wedges)

A classic shortbread from Holland and gloriously rich. If preferred, omit the lemon peel and sift the flour with 1½ teaspoons of allspice.

1. Cream the butter and sugar together until very light and fluffy (the consistency should resemble whipped cream).

2. Stir in the lemon peel, if used, with the flour. Alternatively, sift the spice and flour onto a plate and, using a fork, stir into the creamed mixture.

3. Spread the mixture evenly into a round cake pan 8 or 9 inches in diameter by 1 inch deep.

4. Make a lattice pattern on top with the prongs of a fork, then brush with evaporated milk.

5. Bake for 35 minutes in an oven preheated to 350°F (180°C).

6. Cool in the pan for 10 minutes. Cut into 10 wedges, lift out carefully, and transfer to a wire cooling rack. Store in an airtight tin when completely cold.

1 *cup unsalted butter, softened*

¾ *cup granulated sugar*
Finely shredded peel of 1 washed and dried lemon or

1½ *level teaspoons allspice*

3 *cups all-purpose flour*

Topping
A little unsweetened evaporated milk

1½ cups whole-wheat flour
½ cup all-purpose flour, sifted
Large pinch of salt
3 teaspoons ground ginger
1 teaspoon baking powder
½ cup butter
¾ cup light brown sugar

GRASMERE SHORTBREAD

(10 wedges)

Grasmere is situated in the Lake District, one of the most beautiful and visually compelling parts of northwest England. Beloved by such eminent poets and writers as William Wordsworth and Thomas De Quincy for its peace, tranquillity, and scenic drama, Grasmere is justifiably famous as a tourist resort and for a special type of gingery shortbread that dates from the mid-seventeenth century.

1. Sift the flours, salt, ginger, and baking powder into a bowl.

2. Rub in the butter or margarine with the fingertips until finely blended. Add the sugar.

3. Sprinkle thickly into an 8-inch-round, 1-inch-deep, buttered cake pan, tapping pan lightly to form an even layer.

4. Smooth the top by pressing lightly downward with the flat of the hand.

5. Bake in an oven preheated to 300°F (150°C). Allow about 45 minutes, or until the shortbread is firm and pale gold.

6. Cool to lukewarm in the pan, then cut into 10 wedges. Carefully remove to a wire rack. Store in an airtight tin when cold.

DUTCH JANHAGEL

(Makes 20)

Dutch cinnamon biscuits are one of the highlights of ordering a cup of coffee in Holland—one of these biscuits nearly always comes with it!

1. Sift the flour and cinnamon into a bowl. Add the sugar.

2. Rub in the butter. Draw the mixture together with a fork.

3. Spread the mixture into a buttered jelly-roll pan measuring about 11 × 7 inches, and smooth with a damp knife or palm of the hand.

4. Sprinkle with almonds and sugar. Bake for 35 minutes, or until golden brown, in an oven preheated to 350°F (180°C).

5. Cool to lukewarm; then cut into 20 fingers. Store in an airtight tin when cold.

1½ cups all-purpose flour
1 teaspoon cinnamon
¼ cup granulated sugar
½ cup unsalted butter

Topping
2 tablespoons almond flakes
1 tablespoon granulated sugar

1 7½-oz. jar stem ginger in
   syrup (available from
   gourmet and Chinese
   food stores)
4 cups self-rising flour
1 cup unsalted butter
1 medium egg, well beaten

Topping
¾ cup whole almonds,
   blanched and slit
   lengthwise into halves

DUTCH GINGER SHORTCAKE

(Makes 24)

For those who like stem ginger, these rich and buttery fingers will
be a sheer delight.

1. Drain the ginger and chop. Reserve the syrup.

2. Sift the flour into a bowl. Rub in the butter. Add half the
chopped ginger.

3. Stir in the reserved syrup and the egg. Work together with a
fork.

4. Spread evenly into a large buttered jelly-roll pan measuring
13 × 9 inches.

5. Press the remainder of the chopped ginger and the nuts on
top. Bake for 30 to 40 minutes, or until light brown, in an oven
preheated to 350°F (180°C).

6. Cool to lukewarm in the pan, then cut into 24 fingers.
Transfer to a wire cooling rack. Store in an airtight tin when
cold.

SAVORY BISCUITS

BACON BISCUITS
(Makes 28 to 30)

A surprise package, quite delicious with midmorning coffee or a cup of tea.

1/2 lb. bacon, finely chopped
3/4 cup butter or margarine
1 1/2 cups all-purpose flour
1 cup shredded Cheddar
    cheese

1. Fry the bacon in its own fat until crisp and golden brown. Drain on paper towels.

2. Beat the butter or margarine until creamy. Using a fork, stir in the flour, cheese, and two-thirds of the bacon.

3. Place 28 to 30 teaspoonfuls of the mixture, well apart so they can spread, onto 2 greased cookie sheets.

4. Sprinkle the rest of the bacon over the biscuits. Bake for 30 minutes in an oven preheated to 325°F (160°C).

5. Transfer to a wire cooling rack. Leave until cold. Can be stored for up to one week in an airtight container in the refrigerator.

1 cup all-purpose flour
¼ teaspoon salt
¼ teaspoon sweet paprika
   Large pinch cayenne
      pepper
   Large pinch garlic powder
¼ cup butter or margarine
1 tablespoon shortening
1 small egg, beaten
   Cold water to mix; if
      necessary

Filling
   Canned tomato paste
   Celery salt

SAVORY TWISTS

(Makes 30)

Appetizing savory biscuits that are ideal for cocktail parties.

1. Sift the dry ingredients into a bowl. Rub in the butter or margarine, and the shortening, with the fingertips until finely blended.

2. Mix to a fairly stiff dough with the egg and water as needed. Turn onto a floured surface. Knead lightly until smooth and wrap in foil or plastic wrap. Refrigerate for 30 minutes.

3. Roll out thinly into a rectangle measuring 12 × 8 inches.

4. Spread thinly with tomato paste to within ½ inch of the edges, then sprinkle lightly with celery salt.

5. Brush the edges with water, then fold the pastry in half to form a rectangle measuring 6 × 8 inches.

6. Press lightly with a rolling pin, then cut into approximately 30 strips, each 3 inches in length.

7. Twist each strip from top to bottom and place on a well-buttered cookie sheet. Bake for about 12 to 15 minutes in an oven preheated to 425°F (220°C).

8. Cool on a wire rack. Store in an airtight tin when cold.

ENGLISH CHEESE ASSORTMENT

Take one recipe and make four different biscuits. This "batch baking" saves a good deal of time and trouble—ideal for busy cooks who may like to spend one day a week in the kitchen cooking and baking for the week, or weeks, ahead.

1. Sift the dry ingredients into a bowl.

2. Rub in the butter or margarine until finely blended. Add the cheese.

3. Mix to a stiff (but not too crumbly) dough with egg yolks and a little water, using a fork to gather the ingredients together.

4. Turn onto a floured surface and knead lightly until smooth.

5. Wrap in foil or plastic wrap and refrigerate for 1 hour.

6. Unwrap and divide the pastry into 4 equal portions.

3 cups all-purpose flour
1 teaspoon salt
1/4 teaspoon white pepper
1 teaspoon dry mustard
1/2 level teaspoon paprika
1 cup butter or margarine
2 cups Cheddar cheese,
  finely shredded
2 egg yolks from medium
  eggs
Cold water

1 *portion of pastry*

CHEESE STRAWS

(*Makes 3 to 4 dozen*)

1. Roll out first portion of pastry thinly. Cut into 36 to 48 strips, 3 inches in length. Arrange strips carefully on lightly greased cookie sheets.

2. Re-roll the pastry trimmings and cut into 2-inch rings with cookie cutters. Place on the sheets.

3. Bake until pale gold, allowing about 7 to 10 minutes in an oven preheated to 450°F (230°C).

4. Remove carefully to wire racks and leave to cool.

5. To serve, thread the straws through the rings to look like bales of hay. Store in an airtight tin.

1 *portion of pastry*

MORNING COFFEE BISCUITS

(*Makes 12 to 14*)

1. Roll out second portion of pastry and cut 12 to 14 rounds with a 2-inch plain cookie cutter. Transfer to 1 or 2 greased cookie sheets.

2. Bake as for Cheese Straws, allowing about 12 minutes.

3. Cool on a wire rack. Store in an airtight tin.

CHEESE BUTTERFLIES

(Makes 12 to 14)

1 portion of pastry

Cheese Cream

3/8 cup butter, softened
1/2 cup Cheddar cheese, very finely shredded
Salt
Pepper
1/2 teaspoon prepared mustard

Topping

Paprika or finely chopped parsley

1. Roll out third portion of pastry thinly and cut into 24 to 28 rounds with a 1-inch plain cookie cutter.

2. Cut 12 to 14 rounds in half to form "wings." Transfer to greased cookie sheets.

3. Bake exactly as for Cheese Straws. Cool on wire racks.

4. To serve, make up cheese cream by beating together the butter, cheese, salt and pepper to taste, and the mustard. Pipe or spoon whorls of the cheese cream onto the whole biscuits; then top with "wings" so they resemble butterflies in flight.

5. Dust lightly with paprika or finely chopped parsley.

CHEESE SANDWICH BISCUITS

(Makes 12 to 14)

1 portion of pastry
Cheese cream, as given for Cheese Butterflies above

1. Roll out fourth portion of pastry thinly and cut into 24 to 28 rounds with a 1-inch plain cookie cutter.

2. Bake exactly as for Cheese Straws. Cool on wire racks.

3. To serve, sandwich together with cheese cream.

2 cups all-purpose flour
½ teaspoon salt
¾ cup butter or margarine
½ cup finely shredded
    Parmesan cheese
½ cup walnuts, finely
    chopped
1 egg yolk from medium egg
1 to 2 tablespoons cold
    water

Topping
1 egg white from medium
    egg

CHEESE AND WALNUT BISCUITS (Makes 32)

Very Italian in character, these are sophisticated, savory biscuits with a deliciously nutty flavor.

1. Sift the flour and salt into a bowl. Rub in the butter or margarine with the fingertips until finely blended. Add two-thirds of the cheese and the same amount of nuts.

2. Using a fork, mix to a stiff dough with egg yolk and water. Draw together to form a ball. Wrap in foil or plastic wrap and refrigerate 1 hour.

3. Roll out on a floured surface to a thickness of ¼ inch. Cut into about 32 rounds with a 2-inch fluted cookie cutter.

4. Transfer to lightly greased cookie sheets. Brush with egg white whipped until just foamy. Sprinkle with the rest of the cheese and nuts.

5. Bake until pale gold, allowing 25 minutes in an oven preheated to 350°F (180°C).

6. Cool on wire racks. Store in an airtight tin when cold.

LUNCH-BOX PEANUT BARS (Makes 12)

Packed with cheese and topped with nuts, these shortbread-style savory bars are perfect for packed meals and should be especially popular with children. Margarine may be used instead of butter, but expect a somewhat different flavor.

3/4 cup butter, softened
2 cups all-purpose flour
1/2 teaspoon dry mustard, sifted
1 1/2 cups Cheddar cheese, finely shredded

Topping
1/2 cup salted peanuts

1. Cream the butter until light. Stir in the flour, mustard, and cheese.

2. Draw the mixture together with the hands. Spread evenly into a jelly-roll pan measuring 11 × 7 inches.

3. Sprinkle with peanuts and press down with the flat of the hand to keep them in position.

4. Bake until pale gold, allowing 45 minutes in an oven preheated to 325°F (160°C).

5. Cool to lukewarm, then cut into 12 bars. Carefully lift onto a wire cooling rack. Store in an airtight tin when cold.

1 cup all-purpose flour
1/2 teaspoon salt
1/4 cup butter
2 to 3 tablespoons cold
    water

Filling
2 ounces blue cheese

DANISH BLUE CHEESE STRAWS (Makes 50)

An original idea from Denmark and a delicious appetizer.

1. Sift the flour and salt into a bowl. Rub in the butter.

2. Mix to a stiff paste with water. Turn onto a floured surface. Knead lightly until smooth.

3. Roll out thinly into a rectangle measuring about 12 × 8 inches.

4. Grate the cheese and use it to coat one-half of the rolled pastry. Fold and cover with the second half.

5. Re-roll the pastry until very thin and the pattern of the cheese just begins to show through.

6. Cut into narrow strips, 3 inches in length. Transfer to buttered cookie sheets.

7. Bake until light brown, allowing about 10 minutes in an oven preheated to 400°F (200°C).

8. Cool on a wire rack. Store in an airtight tin when cold.

DEVILED TRIANGLES (Makes 20)

These are tasty Old English biscuits that can be eaten for supper with wedges of cheese or hard-boiled eggs and salad.

1. Sift all the dry ingredients into a bowl. Rub in the butter or margarine.

2. Add the cheese. Mix to a stiff paste with egg and water.

3. Turn onto a floured surface. Knead lightly until smooth. Divide in half.

4. Roll out each half into a 10-inch round, using a dinner plate as a guide.

5. Cut each circle into 10 triangles. Transfer to 2 well-greased cookie sheets. Brush with egg or milk. Sprinkle with nuts.

6. Bake until light brown, allowing 12 to 15 minutes in an oven preheated to 400°F (200°C).

7. Transfer to wire cooling racks. Store in an airtight tin when cold.

COCKTAIL TRIANGLES (Makes 40)

Make as above, but cut each round into 20 triangles.

2 cups all-purpose flour
1/2 teaspoon curry powder
1 teaspoon dry mustard
1 teaspoon salt
1/2 teaspoon celery salt
1/2 teaspoon paprika
5/8 cup butter or margarine
1/2 cup sharp Cheddar cheese, shredded
1 medium egg, beaten
2 to 3 tablespoons cold water

Topping
Beaten egg or milk
5 tablespoons salted peanuts, finely chopped

2 cups self-rising sweet flour
1 teaspoon sweet paprika
1 teaspoon salt
½ teaspoon onion or celery salt
1⅛ cup quick-cooking oatmeal
¾ cup butter or margarine
1 teaspoon Worcestershire sauce
5 to 7 tablespoons cold water

SAVORY OAT WEDGES

(Makes 10)

A teatime special for children who prefer savory biscuits to sweet ones.

1. Sift the flour, paprika, and both salts into a bowl. Add the oatmeal.

2. Rub in the butter or margarine with the fingertips until finely blended. Mix to a stiff dough with Worcestershire sauce mixed with the cold water. Add a few extra teaspoons of water if the mixture seems rather dry.

3. Spread into a greased round cake pan, 8 × 1 inches. Spread evenly with a knife.

4. Bake for 30 minutes, or until golden, in an oven preheated to 375°F (190°C).

5. Cool to lukewarm in the pan, then cut into 10 wedges. Transfer carefully to a wire rack. Store in an airtight tin when cold.

CHEESY OAT CRISPS (Makes 30)

These very savory biscuits are equally good with a midmorning cup of coffee or a hot drink at night.

1 1/2 cups self-rising flour
1/2 teaspoon dry mustard
1/2 teaspoon salt
1/4 teaspoon white pepper
1/2 cup quick-cooking oatmeal
1/2 cup shortening
1 tablespoon butter or margarine
1/2 cup sharp Cheddar cheese, finely shredded
4 to 5 tablespoons cold milk

1. Sift the flour, mustard, salt, and pepper into a bowl. Add the oatmeal.

2. Rub in the fat and butter or margarine until finely blended; then add the cheese. Using a fork, mix to a stiff dough with the milk.

3. Turn onto a lightly floured board. Knead lightly until smooth and crack-free.

4. Roll out thinly and cut into approximately 30 fingers.

5. Transfer carefully to 2 well-greased cookie sheets.

6. Bake until the biscuits are golden and crisp, allowing 10 to 12 minutes in an oven preheated to 425°F (220°C).

7. Cool on a wire rack. Store in an airtight tin when cold.

1 cup self-rising flour
½ teaspoon salt
½ teaspoon dry mustard
¼ teaspoon freshly ground
    black pepper
¼ teaspoon cayenne pepper
    (hot!)
½ teaspoon paprika
¼ cup butter
¼ cup sharp Cheddar
    cheese, finely shredded
1 egg yolk from medium egg
2 tablespoons cold milk
1 teaspoon Worcestershire
    sauce

Topping

1 egg white from medium
    egg
    Caraway seeds

DEVILED CARAWAY STICKS

(Makes 24)

These rather hot biscuits are excellent served with drinks before a meal.

1. Sift the flour, salt, mustard, peppers, and paprika into a bowl. Rub in the butter until finely blended. Add the cheese.

2. Mix to a stiff dough with the egg yolk, milk, and Worcestershire sauce, beaten together. Draw together with the fingertips.

3. Turn onto a floured surface. Knead lightly until smooth. Roll out thinly. Cut into 24 sticks, each measuring about 6 × 1 inch.

4. Transfer the sticks to greased cookie sheets. Brush with lightly beaten egg white, then sprinkle with caraway seeds.

5. Bake until the biscuits are golden brown and crisp, allowing about 10 minutes in an oven preheated to 400°F (200°C).

6. Remove from the oven and cool on wire racks. Store in an airtight tin when cold.

POPPY SEED SANDWICH BISCUITS   (*Makes 30*)

Appetizing little morsels that go well with an aperitif.

1. Sift the flour, salt, mustard, and both savory salts into a bowl. Add the semolina flour.

2. Rub in the butter or margarine until finely blended. Mix to a stiff dough with the milk, stirring with a fork to draw the ingredients together.

3. Turn onto a lightly floured surface. Knead quickly until smooth. Roll out into a thin oblong.

4. Brush one-half of the pastry with beaten egg. Sprinkle with poppy seeds. Fold over the other half so that the seeds are sandwiched between 2 pieces of pastry.

5. Re-roll thinly. Cut into about 30 rounds with a 1½-inch plain cookie cutter. Transfer to greased cookie sheets. Brush tops with beaten egg.

6. Bake until golden brown and slightly risen, allowing about 12 to 15 minutes in an oven preheated to 375°F (190°C).

7. Cool on a wire rack. Store in an airtight container when completely cold.

1½ *cups self-rising flour*
½ *teaspoon salt*
½ *teaspoon dry mustard*
¼ *teaspoon celery salt*
½ *teaspoon onion salt*
4 *tablespoons semolina flour*
½ *cup butter or margarine*
4 *to 5 tablespoons milk*

Filling
Small quantity of beaten egg
1 *level tablespoon poppy seeds*

PETIT FOURS

MOCHA KISSES

(Makes 10)

Rich and luxurious sandwich biscuits for parties marking special occasions like birthdays or weddings.

3/8 cup unsalted butter
3/8 cup granulated sugar
1 cup all-purpose flour
1 tablespoon cocoa powder
1 teaspoon baking powder
1½ tablespoons cold milk

Filling
¼ cup unsalted butter
5/8 cup confectioners' sugar, sifted
4 teaspoons instant coffee powder
3 to 4 teaspoons milk

Topping
Extra confectioners' sugar, sifted

1. To make the biscuits, cream the butter and sugar well together.

2. Sift together the flour, cocoa powder, and baking powder. Using a fork, stir the dry ingredients into the creamed mixture alternately with the milk.

3. Place 20 teaspoonfuls of the mixture, spaced well apart, on buttered cookie sheets.

4. Bake for 20 minutes in an oven preheated to 375°F (190°C). Cool on a wire rack.

5. To make the filling, cream all the ingredients well together.

6. Spread the filling over the flat sides of the biscuits. Sandwich together. Dust with confectioners' sugar.

7. Store for up to 1 week in an airtight container in the refrigerator.

NUTTY CINNAMON CRESCENTS   (*Makes 12*)

Somewhat Middle Eastern in character, these rich little crescents are aromatic and not over-sweet—they simply melt in the mouth!

2 cups all-purpose flour
½ cup butter or margarine
2½ tablespoons granulated sugar
3 to 3½ tablespoons light cream

Filling
5 tablespoons flaked almonds, *lightly toasted*
1 teaspoon cinnamon
1 egg yolk *from medium egg*
1½ tablespoons granulated sugar

Topping
1 egg white *from medium egg, lightly beaten*
Confectioners' sugar

1. To make the pastry, sift the flour into a bowl. Add the butter or margarine and cut it in with a knife.

2. Rub in the butter with the fingertips until the mixture resembles fine breadcrumbs. Add the sugar. Mix to a stiff dough with the cream.

3. Turn onto a floured surface. Knead lightly until smooth. Cut into 2 portions of equal size.

4. Roll out each portion separately into a 10-inch round. Cut each round into 6 triangles with a sharp knife.

5. To make the filling, coarsely chop the nuts, then mix them with cinnamon, egg yolk, and sugar.

6. Spoon equal amounts of the filling onto the widest part of the pastry triangles.

7. Brush the edges of the pastry with water; then roll up each triangle. Curve to form a crescent shape.

8. Place the crescents on a buttered cookie sheet and brush with egg white.

9. Bake for 25 minutes in an oven preheated to 400°F (200°C).

10. Remove from the oven and transfer to a wire cooling rack. Sift sugar over each and eat when cold.

Note
If possible, make and eat these biscuits on the same day.

FLORENTINES

(Makes 12)

These are the most expensive of biscuits to buy, but quite the opposite if homemade. Florentines are always a treat at teatime or if served instead of wafers with after-dinner ice cream sundaes.

3/8 cup butter
5 tablespoons light cream
1 cup confectioners' sugar, sifted
4 tablespoons all-purpose flour
5/8 cup candied citrus peel, finely chopped
2 tablespoons candied cherries, chopped
1/2 cup flaked almonds
1 1/2 teaspoons lemon juice

Coating
4 squares semisweet dark chocolate (4 ounces)

1. Line 2 large, well-buttered cookie sheets with rice paper, making sure there are no gaps. Alternatively, use wax paper or aluminum foil.

2. Place the butter, cream, and sugar in a saucepan. Heat gently until the butter melts.

3. Remove from the heat. Stir in all the remaining ingredients, except the chocolate. Leave until cold.

4. Spoon equal amounts of the mixture onto the prepared sheets, leaving plenty of room between each mound as they spread.

5. Bake for about 10 minutes, or until pale gold, in an oven preheated to 375°F (190°C).

6. Leave to cool to lukewarm. Carefully remove from the trays and trim away the ragged edges of the rice paper. Cool completely on wire racks.

7. To make the coating, break up the chocolate. Melt it slowly in a basin over hot water.

8. Spread the coating over the rice-paper sides of the Florentines and leave until half-set. Mark in wavy lines with the prongs of a fork.

9. Return to wire racks. Leave until the chocolate has set completely before eating.

10. Store in an airtight tin in a cool place.

FLORENTINE PETIT FOURS

(Makes 24)

For tiny biscuits that you can serve with coffee after a meal, drop 24 mounds of the mixture onto prepared trays. Bake and coat with chocolate as directed above.

SPECIALTY BISCUITS

VIENNA BISCUITS

(Makes 20)

A very special treat for very special occasions.

3/4 cup butter, softened
3/4 cup hazelnuts, finely ground
1/4 cup confectioners' sugar, sifted
1 1/2 cups flour, sifted

Coating

4 squares semisweet dark chocolate (4 ounces)
1 tablespoon butter
3 teaspoons instant coffee powder dissolved in 3 teaspoons hot water

1. Beat the butter until creamy. Stir in the nuts, sugar, and flour, using a fork to mix well.

2. Draw the mixture together and wrap in foil or plastic wrap. Chill in the refrigerator for 1 hour.

3. Roll out thinly on a floured surface. Cut into about 20 rounds with a 3-inch cookie cutter, re-rolling and re-cutting the trimmings to give the required amount.

4. Transfer to cookie sheets. Bake for 20 minutes in an oven preheated to 325°F (160°C). Cool on a wire rack.

5. To coat, melt the chocolate and butter in a basin over hot water. Stir in the coffee.

6. Spread the coating over the biscuits. Leave to set before eating. When cold, store in an airtight tin away from heat.

2 egg whites from large eggs
1 cup ground almonds
1/2 cup granulated sugar
1 tablespoon cornstarch
1/2 teaspoon almond extract
1/2 teaspoon vanilla extract

Topping
6 to 7 blanched almonds, split lengthwise
A little extra egg white

MACAROONS

(Makes 12 to 14)

Traditional and almond-packed, macaroons are still a great favorite in England. They are perfect for Easter and Christmas, when a dozen or so boxed prettily makes a thoughtful gift.

1. Brush 2 large cookie sheets with melted butter. Line completely with rice paper, wax paper, or aluminum foil, making sure there are no gaps.

2. Lightly whisk the egg whites but do *not* allow them to stiffen. Stir in the remaining main ingredients. Mix well.

3. Pipe or spoon small mounds of the mixture onto the prepared sheets. Flatten the mounds slightly with a damp knife.

4. Brush with beaten egg white. Top each mound with an almond half.

5. Bake for 20 to 25 minutes in an oven preheated to 325°F (160°C). When ready, the macaroons should be a light gold color.

6. Cool slightly on the trays; then lift off.

7. Trim away the surplus rice paper (which will look ragged) from around the edge of each macaroon; then cool on a wire rack. Store in an airtight tin when cold.

DANISH BISCUIT SELECTION

Danish housewives are well known for their baking, and here is a selection of typical and traditional biscuits to augment the biscuit tin. They are best when made with Danish butter, but any unsalted butter, or margarine, should give satisfactory results.

BASIC BUTTER BISCUITS   (Makes 54)

This is a basic recipe for 2 varieties of biscuits.

1. Sift the flour and baking powder into a bowl. Rub in the butter with the fingertips until the mixture resembles fine breadcrumbs.

2. Add the sugar to the rubbed-in ingredients. Using a fork, mix to a fairly stiff dough with the vanilla extract, egg, and milk, if necessary.

3. Turn onto a lightly floured surface. Knead until smooth. Divide into 2 equal portions.

2 cups all-purpose flour
3/4 teaspoon baking powder
3/4 cup butter
1/2 cup granulated sugar
1/2 teaspoon vanilla extract
1 large egg, well beaten
Cold milk, if necessary

1 *portion of basic biscuit dough*

Topping
Beaten egg

3 tablespoons blanched almonds, finely chopped

1½ tablespoons granulated sugar

1½ teaspoons cinnamon

HANUKKAH CAKES

Almonds and cinnamon are a Middle Eastern combination widely used in cakes and cookies—and never better than in these confections for Hanukkah, the Jewish wintertime festival of dedication. This recipe comes to us via Denmark.

1. Roll out the dough very thinly on a floured surface. Cut into 33 rounds with a 2-inch plain cookie cutter, re-rolling and re-cutting trimmings to make required quantity.

2. Transfer to lightly buttered cookie sheets. Brush with egg; then sprinkle with almonds, sugar, and cinnamon.

3. Bake for 8 to 9 minutes in an oven preheated to 375°F (190°C). When ready, the cakes should be a light gold color.

4. Cool on a wire rack. Store in an airtight tin when cold.

VANILLA RINGS

(Makes 33)

1 portion of basic biscuit dough
3 tablespoons butter
3 tablespoons ground almonds
3/4 teaspoon vanilla extract

1. Place the dough in a bowl and knead in the rest of the ingredients to form a soft dough.

2. Transfer to an icing bag fitted with a star-shaped pipe.

3. Pipe 33 rings of mixture, each about 2 inches in diameter, onto lightly buttered cookie sheets.

4. Bake until the rings are a light gold, allowing about 9 minutes in an oven preheated to 375°F (190°C).

5. Cool on a wire rack. Store in an airtight tin when cold.

5/8 cup butter, softened
1/4 cup granulated sugar
1 cup all-purpose flour
1/2 cup self-rising flour
2 tablespoons cornstarch
1/4 teaspoon vanilla extract

Topping
  Granulated sugar

DANISH BUTTER FANS

(Makes 24)

Melt-in-the-mouth biscuits for special occasions.

1. Place all the ingredients in a bowl. Work together with the fingers until the mixture holds together and forms a dough. Wrap in foil or plastic wrap and refrigerate for 1 hour.

2. Divide the dough into 3 equal pieces. Roll each out into a 7-inch circle, using a plate as a guide.

3. Cut each round into 8 triangles. Transfer carefully to floured cookie sheets.

4. Dust the tops with sugar. Bake for 15 to 20 minutes, or until pale gold, in an oven preheated to 325°F (160°C).

5. Leave for 5 minutes, then remove carefully to wire racks. Store in an airtight tin when cold.

PETTICOAT TAILS

(Makes 24)

Roll out the three 7-inch rounds as described above. Cut out the centers with a 1-inch plain cookie cutter. Ridge the outside edges with the prongs of a fork. Cut each round into 8 triangles or "petticoats." Bake as above.

DANISH CHOC COOKIES (Makes 40)

Easy-to-make cookies, decorated attractively with candied cherries.

⅝ cup butter, softened
⅝ cup confectioners' sugar, sifted
1½ cups all-purpose flour
1 medium egg, beaten
½ cup chocolate chips
½ cup shelled but unskinned almonds, chopped

Topping
10 candied cherries, quartered

1. Lightly cream together the butter and sugar. Stir in all the remaining ingredients, except the cherries. Mix well together.

2. Place 40 teaspoonfuls of the mixture onto lightly buttered cookie sheets. Keep the mounds well apart as they spread. Top each with a cherry quarter.

3. Bake until they are a warm gold color, allowing about 10 to 12 minutes in an oven preheated to 400°F (200°C). Cool slightly.

4. Remove to a cooling rack. Store in an airtight tin when cold.

3/8 cup butter, softened
Pinch of salt
1 cup all-purpose flour
2 tablespoons confectioners'
     sugar, sifted

Topping
10 almonds, blanched and
     slit lengthwise

DANISH OPTIMIST "CAKES"

(Makes 20)

A lovely name for these crunchy, delicate-tasting cookies topped with almonds.

1. Work all the main ingredients together in a bowl to form a paste.

2. Place 20 small mounds of the mixture onto lightly buttered cookie sheets. Keep the mounds well apart—they spread out during baking.

3. Stud the top of each mound with half an almond.

4. Bake until lightly browned in an oven preheated to 400°F (200°C). Allow about 10 minutes.

5. Cool on a wire rack. Store in an airtight tin when cold.

DANISH RUM RINGS

(Makes 25 to 30)

These crispy rings can be grouped together in fours and tied onto the Christmas tree.

½ cup butter, softened
1½ cups all-purpose flour, sifted
¼ cup confectioners' sugar, sifted
1 egg yolk from small egg
1 to 1½ tablespoons dark rum

Topping
1 egg white from small egg
¼ cup walnuts, finely chopped
3 tablespoons granulated sugar

1. Place all the main ingredients in a bowl. Knead together with the fingertips to form a dough.

2. Wrap the dough in foil or plastic wrap. Refrigerate for 30 minutes. Roll out thinly on a floured surface.

3. Cut into rounds with a 3-inch cookie cutter. Remove the centers with a 1-inch cookie cutter. Re-roll and re-cut the trimmings to make 25 to 30 rings.

4. Transfer to buttered trays. Brush with lightly whisked egg white. Sprinkle with nuts and sugar.

5. Bake until golden brown, allowing about 10 minutes in an oven preheated to 400°F (200°C).

6. Cool on a wire rack. Store in an airtight tin when cold.

1½ cups all-purpose flour
2 tablespoons cocoa powder
3 teaspoons instant coffee
   powder
⅜ cup confectioners' sugar
¾ cup butter, softened

MOCHA SHORTIES

(Makes 16)

These are crisp, rich cookies that need careful handling. Don't attempt to make them on a hot day.

1. Sift the flour, cocoa, coffee powder, and sugar into a bowl. Don't attempt to make them on a hot day.

2. Cream the butter until light. Using a fork, stir in the sifted ingredients.

3. Draw the mixture together and wrap in foil or plastic wrap. Refrigerate for 2 hours or until firm.

4. Turn onto a floured surface. Cut into 16 rounds with a floured knife. Transfer to ungreased cookie sheets.

5. Bake until the cookies are a light gold color, allowing about 20 minutes in an oven preheated to 325°F (160°C).

6. Remove to a wire rack and leave until completely cold before storing in an airtight tin.

ORANGE SHORTIES

(Makes 16)

Follow the recipe above, omitting the coffee and adding 2 level teaspoons finely grated orange peel to the sifted dry ingredients.

BRANDY SNAPS

(Makes 16)

These are delicious, either on their own or filled with whipped cream. Allow plenty of time because Brandy Snaps require patience and attention.

¼ cup butter or margarine
¼ cup dark brown sugar
3 tablespoons light corn syrup
½ cup all-purpose flour
1 teaspoon ground ginger
2 teaspoons lemon juice

1. Place the butter or margarine, sugar, and syrup in a saucepan. Stand over a low heat until the fat and syrup have melted.

2. Sift together the flour and ginger. Add to the melted ingredients along with the lemon juice. Stir well.

3. Place only 4 teaspoonfuls of the mixture onto a large, greased cookie sheet, leaving plenty of room for spreading.

4. Bake for 8 minutes in an oven preheated to 325°F (160°C). Remove the snaps from the oven and leave for no more than 30 seconds to firm up slightly.

5. Lift up each one with a spatula. Roll quickly and loosely round the buttered handle of a wooden spoon. Leave until firm. Slide off onto a wire rack.

6. Use up all the mixture in the same way, to make about 16 Brandy Snaps. Should the unrolled snaps cool down too much and become brittle, return them to the oven to soften for a minute or two. Store in an airtight tin when cold.

2 cups all-purpose flour
Pinch of salt
¼ teaspoon allspice
½ cup unsalted butter
½ cup light brown sugar
1 level teaspoon caraway
   seeds
1 medium egg
½ teaspoon vanilla extract
2 tablespoons sweet sherry

SHREWSBURY EASTERTIDE "CAKES" (Makes 24)

These Eastertide "cakes" were mentioned in the *Ingoldsby Legends*, fantasy stories written in comic verse by the witty Reverend R. H. Barham. They appeared for the first time in the mid-nineteenth century in a publication called *Bentley's Miscellany*.

1. Sift the flour, salt, and allspice into a bowl. Rub in the butter until finely blended. Add the sugar and caraway seeds.

2. Beat the egg thoroughly with the vanilla extract and sherry. Add to the ingredients in the bowl.

3. Using a fork, mix to a soft dough. Wrap in foil or plastic wrap. Refrigerate for 45 minutes.

4. Form into 24 small balls. Arrange on 3 cookie sheets lined with wax paper or foil, first lightly greased.

5. Press flat with the base of a tumbler dipped in flour, then prick with a fork.

6. Bake until light brown, allowing 15 to 20 minutes in an oven preheated to 350°F (180°C).

7. Cool on a wire rack. Store in an airtight tin when cold.

SEDGEMOOR EASTER "CAKES" (*Makes 24*)

A speciality of southwest England, this recipe was originally made for Easter.

1. Sift the flour, spice, and salt into a bowl. Rub in the butter until finely blended.

2. Add the sugar and currants.

3. Beat the egg and brandy well together. Using a fork, stir into the rubbed-in mixture to form a fairly stiff dough.

4. Enclose the dough in foil or plastic wrap and refrigerate for about 30 minutes.

5. Roll out thinly and cut into 24 rounds with a 2-inch cookie cutter.

6. Arrange on greased sheets. Bake until lightly browned in an oven preheated to 350°F (180°C).

7. Transfer to a wire rack. Store in an airtight tin when cold.

---

2 cups all-purpose flour
1 teaspoon allspice
1/4 teaspoon salt
1/2 cup unsalted butter
1/2 cup light brown sugar
1/2 cup dried currants or raisins
1 medium egg
2 tablespoons brandy

2 cups all-purpose flour
1 teaspoon baking powder
½ cup butter or margarine
¾ cup granulated sugar
1 teaspoon vanilla extract
1 medium egg, beaten
A few teaspoons cold
milk, if necessary

REFRIGERATOR COOKIES

(Makes 40)

This version of Refrigerator Cookies is basic and fairly plain, but variations follow should you wish a fancier cookie.

1. Sift the flour and baking powder into a bowl. Rub in the butter or margarine until finely blended. Add the sugar.

2. Mix to a fairly stiff dough with extract, egg and milk, if necessary.

3. Knead the dough until smooth. Shape into a long sausage shape, 2 inches in diameter. Wrap in foil or plastic wrap and twist the ends to seal. Refrigerate for up to 1 week.

4. To bake, unwrap the roll and cut off as many cookies as you want to bake—or use the full quantity. Make sure the slices are fairly thin.

5. Place the slices on a greased cookie sheet, allowing room between each for spreading. Bake the cookies until they are a light gold, allowing 10 to 12 minutes in an oven preheated to 375°F (190°C).

6. Cool on a wire rack. Store in an airtight tin when cold.

CHOCOLATE SPECKLE BISCUITS

(Makes 40)

Make as basic recipe, adding ½ cup shredded semisweet chocolate with the sugar.

ORANGE WALNUT BISCUITS

(Makes 40)

Make as basic recipe, adding ½ cup very finely chopped walnuts and 2 level teaspoons finely grated orange peel with the sugar. Omit the vanilla extract.

LEMON COCONUT BISCUITS

(Makes 40)

Make as basic recipe, adding ½ cup dried flaked coconut and 2 level teaspoons finely grated lemon peel with the sugar. Omit the vanilla extract.

SPICY CHERRY BISCUITS

(Makes 40)

Make as basic recipe, sifting 2 level teaspoons allspice with the flour. Add ¼ cup very finely chopped candied cherries with the sugar. Omit the vanilla extract.

ACKNOWLEDGMENTS

Cadbury Typhoo

Danish Food Centre

Dutch Dairy Bureau

Dutch Wheelbarrow Butter

Edward Billington (Sugar)

English Egg Marketing Board

Elsenham Preserves

English Country Life Butter

English Flour Advisory Bureau

Gale's Honey

Garraways Jams

McDougalls Flour

Progress Bakeware

Snappies Paper Products

INDEX